OSAGE

the
Letters
in
Limerick

By T. Melis

Illustrated by Lisa Voth

For Sophi

Special thanks to Cameron Pratt for his support of this project since day one, for his expertise in the Osage language, and for the many hours he has spent patiently editing and instructing me. This book would not exist without him.

A big thank you to Mark Pearson, Addie Hudgins, and the Osage Language Department who generously donated their time and expertise to help make this book possible.

Thanks to Vann Bighorse, Herman Sleeper, and the Wahzhazhe cultural center for your cultural experience and assistance.

And thank you to Chief Geoffrey Standing Bear and Christian Johnson. Your blessing and encouragement is what finally pushed me to finish this book and bring it to print after many years of work.

And last, but not least, special thanks to my illustrator, Lisa Voth, for the countless hours she devoted to this project with no expectation of reimbursement of any kind. I wish everyone could be lucky enough to have a friend like her!

One hundred percent of any proceeds which may result from the sale of this book will be donated to further the preservation of the Osage language and culture.

ʕ

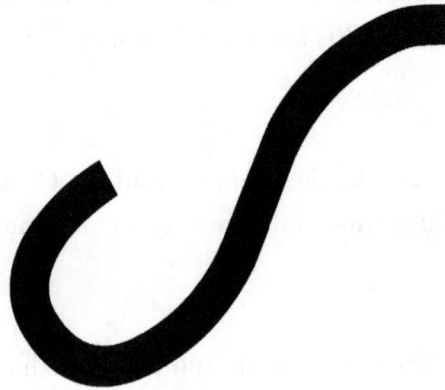

Here's my new friend, we just met!
But now what do we say?
I look at him,
he looks at me,
and then we say ᏒᎡᎻᎪ!

(ha-*weh*)

ƚʒ

Mary has a little ƚʒ̋,
(hkeh)
His shell is hard as rock;
He stops and stares,
and says "Who's there?",
when she says "Knock, knock, knock!"

Đ

I ate a yellow ÐÓZΛ𝕂α,
(***do***-zhon-keh)
and tossed away the peel;
My brother slipped,
and then he tripped,
and fell, head over heels!

O

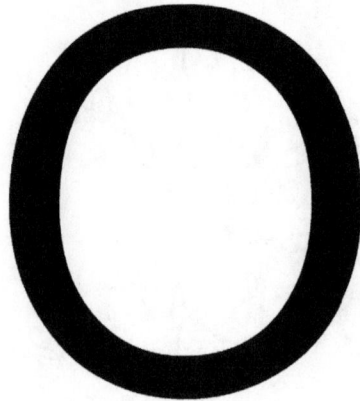

My ӧⅽⲗⲕⲁ is tall and thin,
(***oh***-lan-keh)
My friend's is short and wide;
We look so fine,
That we don't mind,
That we can't fit inside!

Some &őka go "Woof, woof, woof!"

(**shon**-keh)

Some say "Arf!" or "Bark!"

But my &őka,

will only say,

"May we go to the park?"

Þ

ÞⱢ&ⱦⱭⱩⱢ is my favorite fruit,

(baas-**tsek**-a)

Why is that, you say?

They're red and sweet,

A perfect treat,

That always makes my day!

I met a hungry ꝯꝆꞒꞀꝊα,
(wa-*sa*-beh)
I cried out "Please don't eat me!"
He said, "My dear,
please have no fear,
I only eat chop suey!"

Λ

I'm feeling around to find my Ἄϲῆ

(**ah**-leen)

Because I cannot see,
Since my glasses broke…
Ahh! Here we go!
Now, where can my dog be?

I watched a little ǯάοǥˈʌ,
(**htseh**-o-kah)
His big eyes tracked a fly;
His tongue went "slurp!",
I heard a GULP!
The fly went "bzz, bzz….bye"!

Ꮞ

My grandfather is GᎳᎫᎪ,
(*cha*-hpa)
Which means he's short and round.
He won't buy a car;
When he wants to go far,
He just rolls around the town!

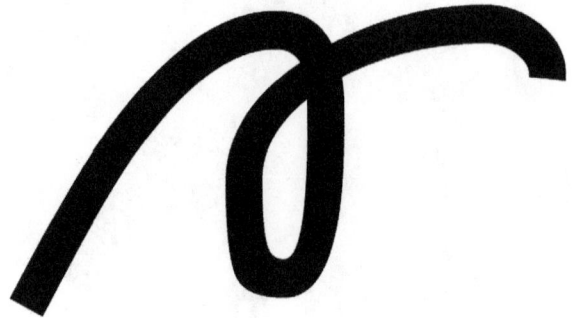

I look up into the sky,
The ᒦᐅᐱᐊ shines bright;
(*mee*-ohn-pah)
I blink my eyes,
In shocked surprise,
Because it's not the night!

D

My friends and I played baseball,
With a ᎹᎠᎠᏔᎠ for a ball;
(wad-*xahn*)
One boy pitched,
The bat went "swish!"
And seeds rained on us all!

α

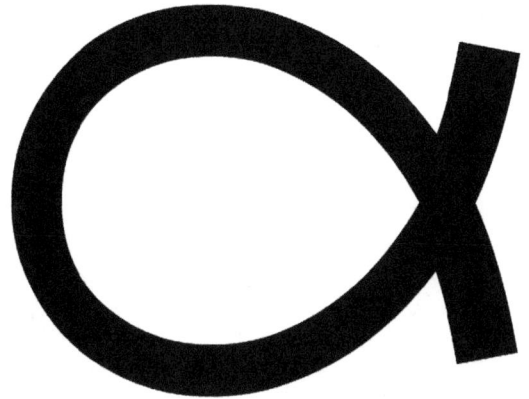

You and I are both ᾱλ́,
(*eh-**na***)
It means we're completely unique.
There's nobody who
is more you than you,
And no one who's "me"-er than me!

I have a little CÚᵏʌÐᴬ́,

(sooka-*dan*)

I think he's a little mixed up!

He follows me 'round,

Buries bones in the ground,

And **barks** when he sees a cute pup?!

U

When I dream at night, I become a ⭢ÚꝪ∧

(*hxoo*-tha)

With my wings spread, I soar through the skies.
When I'm high in the air,
Everything that's down there
Shrinks down to specks in my eyes

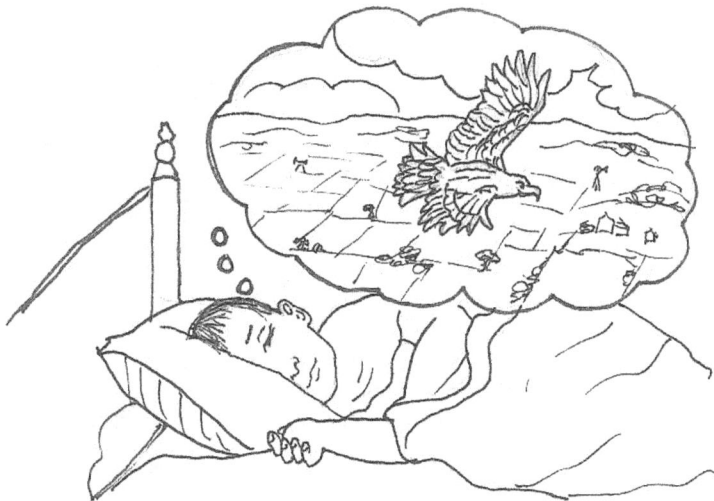

Ƶ

I thought it'd be cool to adopt a ZΛÞα

(*zha*-peh)

With big teeth, and tail black and flat;
But look, over there,
What he did to my chair!
Next time I'll just get a cat…

Today I will only walk ⵜⵍⵟⵍ,
(**ha**-tha)
So I cannot see where I go;
I see where I've been…
Ouch! That was my shin!
Maybe *that's* why mom said "Take it slow!"

ʖ

"Please put sugar in my tea,"
"Thank you, my dear," said Grandma.
She took one sip,
Gasped, and spit;
I think you used ʌ̃ʧ̃ʊɑ!

(**nee**-skoo-eh)

ㄴ

I asked my brother for some ㄴㄲ

(nee)

to quench my thirst; instead,
He took a cup,
filled it up,
and dumped it on my head!

ƕ

The baby twins both want that toy;
Now, what will they do?
"ƕÓRᴧ!", he says;
(*hkon*-bra)
"ƕÓRᴧ!", she says;
And "RIP!" It split in two!

I have a pair of ꙅᴀ́ꞣα,
(**sha**-keh)
With five fingers on each side;
But which is left,
And which is right,
I never can decide!

Ʀ

Now, let me count my fingers;
Will you count with me?
Five on the left,
(or is that the right?)
They add up to Cᴀ́ꞣᴀ́, you see!
(**leh**-bran)

O▪

For my birthday, I asked for an ΠⲤÓαⱫΠ.

(ee-**lon**-ezhee)

Well, I don't mean to be a bother;
He's got paws and whiskers,
But what I had pictured,
Was just a *wee* bit smaller!

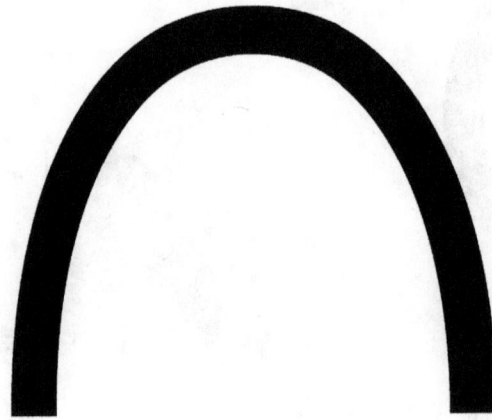

I mixed up the word for ᏂᏓ

(*nee*-da)

I thought I was counting sheep;
Boom! Crash!
Thump! Smash!
Well, this isn't helping me sleep!

7

"I spy something 7ႶႶ," she said,
(zee)
"Guess what it is! Right there!"
I searched around,
and up and down;
I found it! It's my hair!

Ћ

"ᎭᏅᎠᎠ ᎭᏅᎩᎠ!", my uncle warned;
(*thee*-hda-theen-*ka*)
I wish I would have listened!
With one big bite,
It latched on tight...
I guess I learned my lesson!

Ꝥ

I meant to comb my ꝤΛʃŰ,
(hpa-***hoo***)
But forgot it again and again;
As days turned to weeks,
I began to hear cheeps…
Eek! A family of birds has moved in!

Who ate my ꝅꮿ̋ꮯⲁ ōⲥꮮ̃?

(**hka**-tseh o-**lan**)

Let's solve this mystery!

Was it you? Or you?

Let's look for a clue!

Now who do you think it could be?

O

As I walk the path of life,
The road will twist and turn;
Around each bend,
Each OᏢᎯᏍᎤ
(oh-**pa**-shon)
Are lessons to be learned.

Λ̇

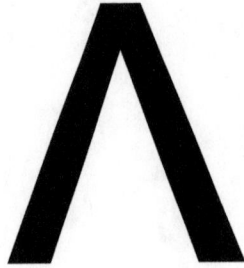

At ʃΛ́, when I look up
(ha^)
at stars twinkling up high;
I think of all
Who've gone before
And seen the same vast sky

I see the warriors hunting ɣɑ̋,
(htse)

A great ꝁʌʃɳ̍ꝁɑ stands,
(ga-*hee*-geh)
proud and tall,
Above them all,
The ruler of the lands

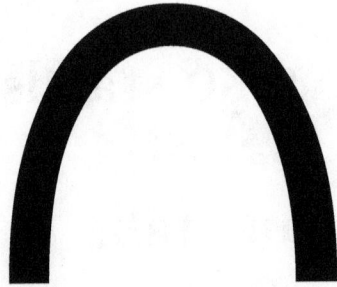

If every n̊ on Earth were a hug,

(een)

and the flowers were kisses, too;

I'd travel around,

and hunt them down,

and give them all to you!

GLOSSARY OF OSAGE WORDS

𐓇𐓘𐓻𐓚	hello
𐓏𐓚	turtle
𐓸𐓘𐓻𐓥𐓶𐓘	banana
𐓷𐓒𐓥𐓶𐓘	hat
𐓮𐓘𐓶𐓘	dog
𐓒𐓮𐓸𐓘𐓶𐓇	strawberry
𐓻𐓇𐓓𐓘𐓒𐓘	bear
𐓘𐓒𐓚	chair
𐓒𐓘𐓶𐓸'𐓇	frog
𐓚𐓘𐓒𐓇	short, squat, rounded
𐓅𐓚𐓷𐓒𐓇	moon
𐓻𐓇𐓓𐓺𐓘	squash
𐓘𐓥𐓘	the only one
𐓒𐓶𐓶𐓇𐓸𐓘	turkey
𐓺𐓶𐓶𐓇	eagle
𐓻𐓘𐓒𐓘	beaver
𐓺𐓘𐓶𐓇	backwards
𐓥𐓘𐓒𐓤𐓶𐓘	salt
𐓥𐓘	water
𐓏𐓘𐓒𐓇	I want it

ȣΛ̋ķα	hands
cά̇RΛ̇	ten
ΩcÓ̇αʎΩ	cat
ʎΩ̋DΛ	elephant
7Ω	yellow
ЂΩ̄ĐΛ́̇ ЂΩ̇ķΛ́	Don't touch!
ÞΛJŰ	hair
ķΛ̋ƻα ŌcΛ́̇	pie
JΛ̋̇	night
ƻα̋	buffalo
ķΛJΏķα	chief
Ω̇	rock